CONTENTS

THE CHANCTONBURY CRASHES

© Copyright Martin F. Mace, 1998.

Published 1998 by the Historic Military Press,
Green Arbor, Rectory Road, Storrington, West Sussex, RH20 4EF.

ISBN 1 901313 02 02.

Printed in the United Kingdom by BDA Associates,
Unit T, Rich Industrial Estate, Avis Way, Newhaven, East Sussex, BN9 0DJ.
Telephone 01273-516566.

INTRODUCTION

Early on the 3rd February 1940, a British convoy at sea off the Yorkshire Coastline was attacked by Heinkel He-111s of KG26 operating from Schlewsig.

Directed by the radar station at Danby Beacon, Hurricanes from No.43 Squadron went to the aid of the convoy. In the following battle, one of the Heinkels was shot down by Flight Lieutenant (later Group Captain) Peter Townsend, and crashed in the winter snow at Sneaton Castle.

This was the first German aircraft to be destroyed in the skies over England since the First World War. It was by no means to be the last. On the 10th July 1940, the period officially known as the Battle of Britain commenced. By its end some 82 days later almost every corner of the United Kingdom would have been touched by the effects of this enormous aerial battle.

The Chanctonbury District was no exception. Even today many local people can still vividly recall the contrails and noise of the confused dogfights. This book is the story of five German aircraft that crashed in the Chanctonbury area during the Battle of Britain. These aircraft do not represent the total of the wartime crashes in this area, but are described here by virtue of a photograph that appeared in a national aviation magazine in 1987. This picture showed a Messerschmitt Bf-109 that had crashed on the airfield at Parham on the 9th September 1940. This photograph was the initial spark for the research, which not only led to contact with the pilot of this plane, but also with a local resident Geoff Goatcher. As a young schoolboy, Geoff lived in the Chanctonbury area throughout the Battle of Britain. On hearing of a crashed plane, Geoff would jump on his bicycle and cycle to the crash site. Here he would sketch what he saw, providing us with a unique source of information on many of the crashes included within this book.

FRIDAY 16TH AUGUST 1940

Friday the 16th was a typical sunny summer's day with just the amount of haze that the German pilots appreciated. The plotting tables had remained quiet until about 11am when a series of raids began to be levelled against Norfolk, Kent and Greater London. At this stage of the Battle of Britain the airfields were still the main target, and on this day Manston and West Malling came in for particular attention.

Shortly after midday, the radar stations spread along the South Coast were displaying a more ominous picture as large German raids began to build up. 50 bombers were heading for the Thames Estuary, 150 appeared off Dover, whilst about 100 were massing off Cherbourg with the intention of making for the Portsmouth and Southampton areas. In all, radar reported over 350 enemy aircraft between Yarmouth and Portland alone!

In response to this threat, Fighter Command dispatched some twelve Squadrons from 10, 11 and 12 Groups. The skies were full of battling aircraft - indeed it was in this melee that Flight Lieutenant James Nicolson of No.249 Squadron won the first Victoria Cross for Fighter Command. Alongside No.249 Squadron in the fight was another of the Tangmere units - No.602 Squadron. In control of a 602 Squadron Spitfire was Flying Officer P.C. Webb.

At about 5.45pm Webb engaged a Messerschmitt Bf-110 of the 3rd Staffel, ZG 76. Like those 110s from the same unit that were to be lost on the 4th September, it had probably been based at the captured French airfield at Laval, Near Abbeville. This particular aircraft carried the aircraft codes of 2N+AP, though its Werke or serial number remains unknown. It was piloted by Oberleutnant (Flying Officer) Urban

Messerschmitt Bf-110
LEE FARM - CLAPHAM

Aircraft Code: **2N ✚ AP**

Werke No.:   N/K
Flight Group: 3rd. Staffel ZG76
Crew: U. Schlaffer (pilot)
               F. Obser

The exact location of the Bf-110 at Lee Farm near Clapham

The site can be seen by heading south from the South Downs Way, along the footpath from Chantry Hill Carpark.

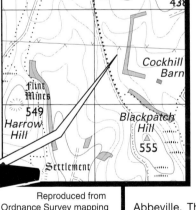

Reproduced from Ordnance Survey mapping with the permission of the Controller of HMSO © Crown Copyright, Licence no. MC 88223M

5

Schlaffer, whilst the co-pilot was Obergefreiter (Leading Aircraftsman) Franz Obser.

During his attack, Webb inflicted what was to be mortal damage to the Bf-110. Finding it difficult to remain airborne the plane staggered eastwards roughly along the northside of the South Downs. As it approached Amberley, the passage of the aircraft was witnessed by Mrs Ethel Woods. At the time Mrs Woods was a housewife living in the cottages alongside Rackham Street in Crossgates, Amberley.

"I was working in the garden when I saw the plane come down. As it first passed overhead, it appeared as if it was going to crash into the side of the Downs, but it actually passed just above Rackham Hill and headed south. I will always remember the size of this aircraft as it had two engines and hence two propellers. I walked with the children up to Springhead Hill from where we could clearly see the crash site. From where I was, the plane appeared in perfect condition with very little damage indeed. Shortly after the Police arrived from Storrington, but we did not see an ambulance or fire engine."

The plane had come to rest on an open field on top of the Downs at Lee Farm, near Clapham. It had suffered only minor damage during the course of the 'belly landing'. Further inspection revealed that the aircraft had no extra armour plating fitted and that the standard armament for a Bf-110 was fitted.

The Supermarine Spitfire. This is not the exact aircraft that shot down the Lee Farm Bf-110, but is similar to the plane that F/O Webb was using at the time.
(Wing Commander H. Randall, DFC).

The wreckage of Messerschmitt Bf-110 2N+AP. The aircraft does appear to be in remarkable condition, with even the cockpit covers still in place. There are, however, the usual bent and twisted propeller blades.
(Mr A. Saunders).

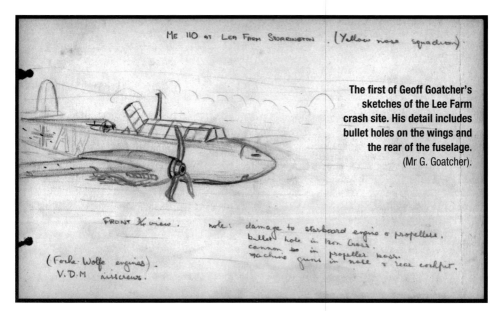

The first of Geoff Goatcher's sketches of the Lee Farm crash site. His detail includes bullet holes on the wings and the rear of the fuselage.
(Mr G. Goatcher).

A couple of days after the crash another visitor, Geoff Goatcher, made his way up to the crash site. He had not witnessed the actual crash itself, but was still determined to examine what was left of the plane.

"It took us a while to walk across the Downs to the plane, but we were surprised on our arrival to see that it was unguarded. The usual army troops or Policeman were nowhere in sight. We immediately took the opportunity to try and extract some souvenirs. We had only just begun when a lorry full of soldiers, I think they were Canadian, arrived by driving across the fields. However, they showed no interest in my cousin and I, but simply set about trying to rip the Swastika from the tailplane!".

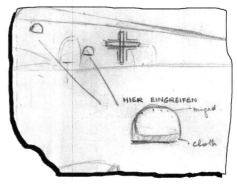

Details of the footsteps on the side of the aircraft's fuselage,
(Mr G. Goatcher).

This fuel heater, currently on display at the Amberley Chalk Pits Museum, is believed to have been 'liberated' from the Lee Farm 110 by a local person seeking a souvenir at the time of the crash.
(Photographed by kind permission of the Directors of the Amberley Chalk Pits Museum).

Another drawing of the whole aircraft, this time a 3/4 view. Here we can see further details of the damage to the aircraft, including oil on the tailplanes. There is also an indication that prior to being shot down themselves the crew had some success in an earlier confrontation! (Mr G. Goatcher).

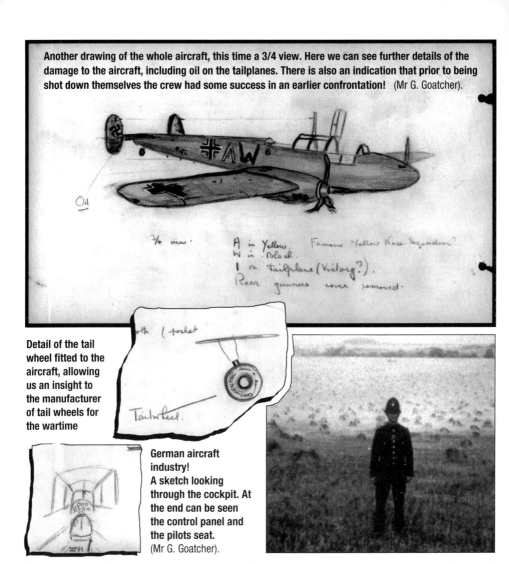

Oil

3/4 view.

A in Yellow.   Famous Yellow Nose Squadron?
W in Black.
1 on Tailplane (Victory?).
Rear gunners cover removed.

Detail of the tail wheel fitted to the aircraft, allowing us an insight to the manufacturer of tail wheels for the wartime German aircraft industry!
A sketch looking through the cockpit. At the end can be seen the control panel and the pilots seat. (Mr G. Goatcher).

A distant view of the crash site. The aircraft is in fact directly above the head of the local policeman on the opposite side of the valley. Note Chanctonbury Ring on the far horizon. Storrington is to the left of the picture, and Worthing some way of on the right. (Mr A. Saunders).

This final sketch for the Lee Farm Bf-110 concentrates more on the detail of one of the wings. (Mr G. Goatcher).

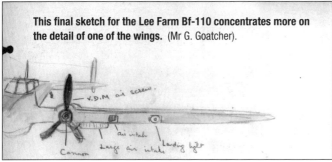

WEDNESDAY 4TH SEPTEMBER 1940

PART 1

Wednesday the 4th of September dawned fine and warm, with a light haze through the English Channel. Despite such pleasant conditions, it was a day during which the skies would be full of hectic air battles, for the Battle of Britain was still well under way. The Luftwaffe had taken to the skies early with the aim of carrying out Goering's directive about making direct attempts to smash Britain's aircraft industry. Attacks were to follow on Lympne, Eastchurch, on an aircraft factory at Rochester, and on the industrial area at Brooklands. During the bombing of the latter, the Vickers factory in particular was to suffer serious damage.

It was roughly midday when one of the first waves of German aircraft crossed the coast. Some 70 odd Heinkel He-111 and Dornier Do-17 bombers escorted by over 200 Messerschmitt Bf-109 and Bf-110 fighters headed north between Hastings and Dover. They then split into five separate groups to make their way to their targets. Another separate group of Bf-110s were reported north of Guildford. These were the aircraft making for the Vickers factory at Brooklands, flying at low level. The final part of this raid was a further gaggle of Bf-110s tasked to attack the radar station at Poling.

Messerschmitt Bf-110
STRIVENS FARM - STEYNING

Aircraft Code: **2N ✠ HM**

Werke No.: 3563
Flight Group: 3rd. Staffel ZG76
Crew: W. Shultis (pilot)
R. Bilbeck

The location of the crash site at what was Strivens Farm, Steyning.

Since the war the whole area of the crash site has been built upon, though the exact site is roughly in the area surrounding the road called 'Portway'.

Reproduced from Ordnance Survey mapping with the permission of the Controller of HMSO © Crown Copyright, Licence no. MC 88223M

With large formations moving in before splitting to attack the various targets, interception was proving a nightmare. The pilots of Fighter Command were by now succumbing to exhaustion, were frequently outnumbered and nearly always had to cede height and position to the German attackers. At about 1.20pm, Pilot Officer H.W. Moody took off in his Spitfire from Westhampnett airfield along with other aircraft from 602 Squadron, including that of its commander Squadron Leader Sandy Johnstone. Climbing to intercept

9

the enemy, (either the group of Bf-110s that had targeted Poling radar station, or the returning Brooklands raiders), P/O Moody described what happened next:

"I broke away after a group of enemy aircraft and then singled out a group of four who were circling and using their machine guns against me. They were at the same height of about 10,000ft. I attacked the near one on full beam and head on. I saw the enemy aircraft crash behind Shoreham".

The aircraft hit by P/O Moody was a Messerschmitt Bf-110 C-4 from 3 Staffel, ZG 76 based at Laval airfield, near Abbeville in Northern France. The Bf-110 was originally designed in 1934 as a long-range escort fighter, with the Bf-110C first entering service in 1939. During the Battle of Britain the shortcomings of the Bf-110 as a fighter were exposed, with losses so heavy that the Luftwaffe became obliged to send the more

agile single engined Bf-109s to protect the Bf-110s!.

Having been hit, this Bf-110 began to lose height, and staggered east in an attempt to make it across the Channel. Geoff Goatcher witnessed its last few minutes:

"I was standing at Windyridge, Washington at about Midday. During what had been a day of hectic air battles, this aircraft appeared flying erratically from west to east. It was between the South Downs and us, at about 500 or 600 feet. From were I was standing it seemed that the plane was below the top of the Downs. At first it appeared to come down at the foot of Chanctonbury Ring, but at the last minute it rose a little and disappeared just over the top of the trees in Wiston Park. It then made a reasonable wheels up crash landing near Wiston Park. With my parents I made my way across to the crash site which was on one of the fields of Strivens Farm in Steyning".

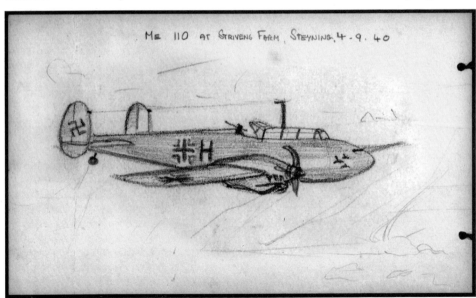

The sketch that Geoff Goatcher made of the Strivens Farm Bf-110. The aircraft carried the code 2N+HM, but in the drawing Geoff has only included the 'H'. In reality, the H was known to have been painted in white. Once again the indications are that the pilot made a good crash landing - the major damage being bent propeller blades. (Mr G. Goatcher).

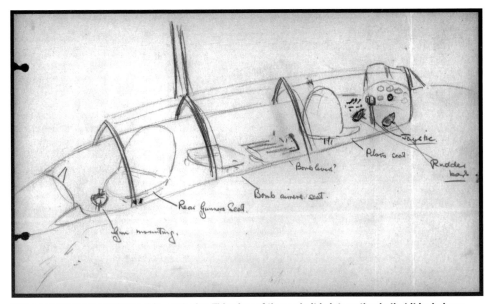

The second sketch relating to this crash site. This view of the cockpit is interesting in that it includes a bomb aimer's seat and the actual bomb release gear. (Mr G. Goatcher).

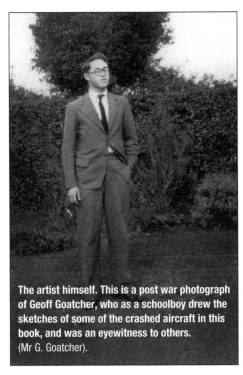

The artist himself. This is a post war photograph of Geoff Goatcher, who as a schoolboy drew the sketches of some of the crashed aircraft in this book, and was an eyewitness to others. (Mr G. Goatcher).

The aircraft had in fact made a near-perfect crash landing. Its crew, Unteroffizer (Corporal) W. Schultis and Unteroflizer R Bilbeck, both walked away from the crash with only minor injuries and were taken prisoner.

Detailed reports made by both the R.A.F. and the Police after the crash go on to describe the aircraft in detail. On the side of the fuselage it carried the coding of 2N+HM, with the 'H' having been painted in white. Stencilled on the fin was the Werke (serial) number 3563, and four sets of dates, no doubt indicating earlier successes over the R.A.F - 12.08.40; 13.08.40; 15.08.40 and 1.9.40. The aircraft was fitted with the standard Daimler-Benz DB.601 engines, and on each spinner were a series of painted white rings. Further examination revealed that the aircraft was not fitted with any armour plating and that it was armed with standard weapons for this aircraft - two 20mm cannon and four 7.9mm machine guns in the fuselage nose, and a sole 7.9mm machine-gun in the rear of the cockpit.

On his arrival at the crash site, Geoff Goatcher watched as the military set up a guard on the plane, as well as marching the two crew off to captivity. The plane was eventually removed by an R.A.F. salvage crew from 49 Maintenance Unit based at Faygate Railway Station north of Horsham. Unlike the crew of this plane, Pilot Officer Moody was not so lucky. He was killed in action only 3 days later on the 7th, one of 19 R.A.F. fighter pilots to lose their lives on the day that is often described as the Armageddon of the Battle of Britain.

A view of the crash site looking north from the South Downs, with Chanctonbury Ring to the left of this picture. The actual crash site cannot be pinpointed, but is known to be roughly where the grass area can be seen in the middle of the houses.
(Authors collection).

WEDNESDAY 4TH SEPTEMBER 1940

PART 2

From his vantage point at Washington, this was not the only aircraft crash that Geoff Goatcher was to witness that day. At almost the same time that the 110 crashed at Steyning, he was to see yet another of this type fall to earth nearer to home at Washington. This time, however, the crash was more dramatic.

This Messerschmitt Bf-110, also from the 3 Staffel ZG76 based at Laval, carried the code lettering 2N+DP and the Werke number 2837. At about the time that Pilot Officer Moody engaged the first Bf-110, this plane was attacked by Squadron Leader Ceaser Hull. Hull was a South African serving with 43 Squadron flying Hurricanes from Tangmere. Like Pilot Officer Moody, Hull was to be killed before the end of the Battle of Britain.

Messerschmitt Bf-110
CHURCH FARM - WASHINGTON

Aircraft Code: 2N ✠ DP

Werke No.:   2837
Flight Group: 3rd. Staffel ZG76
Crew: Florenz (pilot)
                Herbert

The location of the crash site at what was Church Farm Washington.

The exact location of the crash site is now under the route of the A24, but during the war would have been open farmland.

As Geoff Goatcher describes, the whole engagement was over very quickly:

"Having been hit, the German aircraft went into a very steep, if not vertical dive. It did not recover from this and crashed straight into the ground at Church Farm. The crash was at such speed that the plane buried itself to a depth of about 20ft. Nothing could be seen except the crater, and for this reason I was not able to make sketches of the remains. "

Needless to say with a crash of such speed and violence, the crew did not survive. Both Oberleutnant (Flying Officer) Florenz and Gefreiter (Aircrafts-man First Class) Herbert were killed. Perhaps as a consequence of the nature of the crash, many local people remember the actual location. Mrs Sheila Becher is one of those people:

"The German plane, a fighter as there were only two people in it, was shot down into a

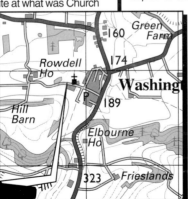

Reproduced from Ordnance Survey mapping with the permission of the Controller of HMSO © Crown Copyright, Licence no. MC 88223M

One of the targets of the German attackers on the 4th of September 1940 was the radar station at Poling. This view shows the three transmitter towers that once stood at this location. (Mrs M. Taylor).

field south of The Drive and below East Holt Wood. The field, then farmed by Mr Turner, is part of Church Farm".

Mr C. Turner also recalls the aftermath of the crash.

"The plane had dived into the ground to at least 12-15ft. Something in the crater was burning as smoke was billowing out - in fact I seem to remember that something kept smouldering for almost two weeks. The whole area was dangerous for, as well as the fire, unexploded bullets kept going off, making sure that spectators were kept at a distance. Having crashed on our land I was eventually able to have a look at the contents of the crater. All that I can recall seeing were a few bent and twisted pistons."

The site now lies under the carriageway of the A24 at about the point were Church Street crosses the dual carriageway. The site was excavated in 1965 by a group of aviation enthusiasts. Both of the plane's DB01 engines were recovered, along with the propellers, undercarriage, manufacturer labels and a host of other small components. Also unearthed at the same time were partial remains of the crew, but nothing to establish their identity beyond any doubt. During later road widening work, construction workers uncovered a complete parachute pack, which may now be found in the private collection of Mr Peter Foote.

Footnote: Even now, the carnage had not ended for the 3rd Staffel ZG76, for on this day they lost two other aircraft in the Chanctonbury area alone. A Messerschmitt Bf- 110 C-4, with the aircraft code 2N+BM, was shot down over High Salvington, Worthing, at 1.25pm. The crew, Oberleutnant Schilier and Feldwebel (Sergeant) Winkler, were both captured.

The second Bf-110, aircraft code 2N+KP and Werke No. 2104, came to earth at Toat Farm, Pulborough. This aircraft had been attacked by 43 Squadron Hurricanes whilst over Wisborough Green and fell inverted and in flames on a hedgerow not far from the Toat Monument. Both of the crew, Oberleutnant Raetsch and Obergefreiter (Leading Aircraftsman) Hemfel, were killed and subsequently buried at St. Mary's Church in Pulborough. A major recovery was carried out in 1973 by the Wealden Aviation Archeological Group. A complete Daimler Benz DB 601 engine was recovered along with a propeller boss, one propeller blade, an undercarriage leg, and parts of the second engine. The date on the casting of the port engine was 23/10/39, whilst that on the starboard was 21/10/37.

The approximate location of the Washington crash is marked by this road bridge, where The Street crosses the A24. In fact it was during the excavation of the road cutting and the building of this bridge that some of the remains of the aircraft were found. (Authors collection).

The Bf-110 that crashed at Washington was shot down by Squadron Leader Ceaser Hull. Hull was serving with 43 Squadron flying Hurricanes from Tangmere. This Hurricane is not that flown by Hull, but a similar type. (Wing Commander H. Randall, DFC).

MONDAY
9TH SEPTEMBER
1940

Monday the 9th September had by 5pm already been a busy day, with the A.R.P. Action Book for West Sussex revealing a long list of occurrences. An unexploded bomb had been reported at Sidlesham; two air raid warnings for Chichester; one at Horsham and four others between Brighton and Worthing; at 5.56pm it was reported that Tangmere was being bombed; and at 6.41pm that a Messerschmitt Bf-109 had come down at Cootham.

This plane was in fact the Messerschmitt Bf-109 E-1 flown by Oberleutnant Erwin Daig, a pilot serving with the 5th Staffel JG27 based at Montreuil on Cap Gris Nez. A full description of the day's events is best illustrated by Oberleutnant Daig himself.

Messerschmitt Bf-109
PARHAM

Aircraft Code: **13** ✠–

Werke No.:   1488/3488
Flight Group: 5th. Staffel JG27
Crew: E. Daig (pilot)

"The task we were given for the 9th of September was relatively simple. We were to act as the escort for the bomber formations whose target were the docks at London. On the return flight, having hit the Channel coast, we were permitted what we called 'free pursuit'. The time of our attack was to be early to mid afternoon.

In finding somewhere to crash, Oberleutnant Daig chose a field that had, and still is, being used as a private airfield. Now used by Southdown Gliding Club, the airfield possesses its own control building and two small hangers.

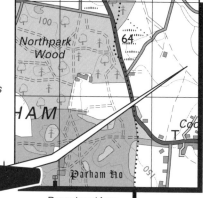

Reproduced from Ordnance Survey mapping with the permission of the Controller of HMSO © Crown Copyright, Licence no. MC 88223M

Having taken off, we quickly took up our assembly positions with the bombers in the skies over St. Omer. A direct course was then set for London. I was one of about 40 Bf-109s, though not all of the fighters were from JG27.

On the approach flight we first made contact with the enemy to the south of the city [London]. Here we mixed with English fighters, there being a fair amount of activity and many short aerial combats. Having dropped our bombs the formation set course for the French Channel coast. However, somewhere in the earlier attacks I must have been hit for I

Oberleutnant Daig, on the right, and a colleague pose for a photograph on their airfield in Northern France, early 1940. It has unfortunately not been possible to establish the type of aircraft behind the two pilots, though it is possible that they are Messerschmitt Bf-109s. (Dr. E Daig).

could not maintain the prescribed speed. As a result of this, and the fact that I had been the last outer right plane, I had begun to trail well behind the rest of the formation. My radio transmitter had also packed up, as I could get no answer from the rest of the formation to my calls.

I then made a mistake that was going to cost me my freedom. Instead of going into a glide, assisted by the engine, and trying to reach the French coast, I maintained my height. At this point two British fighters who had dived down at me from behind on my left-hand side and, from a higher altitude, attacked me. They opened fire, and my plane received more hits. As they did this one of the attackers, possibly a Spitfire, flew past me on my left side. I tried to fire at it and then turned into a steep dive.

During this dive, (the Bf-109 could dive at a greater speed than the Spitfire), I lost contact with my attackers. As I headed over Southern England towards France I tried to reach some broken cloud that I could see at about 3,000 metres. This was another tactical mistake, as before I reached the safety of this cloud, one of my attackers caught up with me and again opened fire. Once again I felt the shock of more hits, at which point I put my plane into yet another dive. This time I kept going until I was almost at ground level, when I headed straight for France, trying to escape by flying at low level.

This went on for a short time, With occasional hits on me by the pursuer. By now my plane had started to smoke, and I was having trouble seeing. I threw back my cockpit hood to see if this would help, but all that happened was that the engine just died! I then saw a gently rising slope, similar to a meadow, that was profusely covered with old lorries. I quickly lost speed and then the plane hit the ground. The chase was finally over!".

17

Here a member of his ground crew helps Oberleutnant Daig through the pre-flight checks. This is the same airfield as the previous picture, but the aircraft is not the one that Oberleutenant Daig crashed at Parham on the 9th September 1940. (Dr. E. Daig).

At about 5.30pm, a Storrington resident, Mr Carpenter, set out on a walk, with the intention of heading off across the fields and woodland that dominates the ground between Storrington and West Chiltington. About fifteen minutes into the walk he began to distinguish the deep growl of aircraft engines.

"Without warning, a Messerschmitt Bf-109 flew overhead. It was very low indeed, being only just above the height of the trees. It was obvious that the plane was going to land. A British fighter which appeared to be a Hurricane immediately followed the Messerschmitt. This aircraft was still firing shots at the Messerschmitt, with some of the rounds hitting the ground in front of me, throwing soil into the air."

As the plane headed from West Chiltington

This aerial shot shows Oberleutnant Daig in a Messerschmitt Bf-109 in the early days of 1940. Again, this is not the aircraft that came to ground at Parham. (Dr. E. Daig).

18

towards its final crash site, it passed over the top of Rydon School and roughly along the course of Thakeham Road in Storrington. At this point the pursuing RAF aircraft were still firing at the 109 as eyewitnesses tell of cartridge shells and bullets falling to the ground, sending people running for cover. Even today in the timberwork of one house in Thakeham Road it is possible to see .303 rounds embedded in the wood.

Nearer the crash site another witness, Mr Waller, had decided to do a spot of fishing. So it was that at 5.45pm he was still attempting to catch his dinner.

"I was standing on the banks of Parham Pond when at about 5.45 I heard the noise of approaching aircraft. The noise grew louder and louder and I looked up just in time to see a Messerschmitt fly very low overhead. In fact it was so low that it only just missed the trees in the estate. Seconds later it was followed by the sound of a crashing aircraft - obviously the 109. I clearly remember the Hurricane that was on the German's tail - making sure that it did actually land!"

Mr Waller at his post behind the headmasters desk of a Storrington School. At the time of the crash Mr Waller was fishing on Parham Pond when the Bf-109 passed overhead at treetop height.
(Mrs J. Ham).

As can be seen from these and other witnesses, Daig had approached Storrington from the north east side, swinging round to the south and finally turning north again into the crash site. Daig had in fact chosen a small private airfield as his crash site. Used pre-war as a private landing strip for the residents of Parham House, the airfield had in the early months of the war been used by Mr Jim Veitch to train local people to become pilots under the Government's Flying Training Scheme. Now used by the Southdown Gliding Club, the airfield is part of Charity Farm, Parham. By September 1940 the large grass field that was the airfield had become festooned with obstacles to prevent a German Invasion.

Even before the plane ended its flight, the emergency services were swinging into action. Mrs Joan Norton (nee Sutcliffe) now lives near Glastonbury in Somerset, but at the time was living with her parents at Roundabout, West Chiltington.

"At the time I was 18 and working as a Red Cross Nurse. I saw the plane pass overhead very low and guessed that it was about to come down nearby. For some reason I thought that it might be Parham. My job was to attend the scene of accidents, and as such I was in my uniform. I jumped into my car, which had been supplied by the Red Cross, and headed for the airfield at Parham. I had made a lucky guess, as I was only the third person to arrive".

When I reached the plane, I immediately saw that it had been shot up. The pilot was sitting on a wing, and I remember thinking how young and terrified he looked. Soon after I arrived, the Home Guard began to appear, along with a growing crowd of local people.

My commandant also turned up and began to check the pilots condition. They had to use sign language as they did not understand each other, but he was able to establish that the pilot only had bruising and mild shock. To carry out these checks my commandant had removed the pilots lifejacket, and as soon as the pilot was removed by the army, he began to walk around the crowd, by now quite large, sporting the life jacket and collecting donations for the Red Cross!.

One other point that I remember about this crash was the fuel. It could be smelt on everything, and in fact small pools of it were lying around the plane. I remember trying to get the pilot away from the plane to prevent the risk of a fire".

As can be seen from his commentary, Daig was under the impression that he had been attacked by two Spitfires. In fact it was not until 1987 that he was to finally learn that they

had been Hurricanes. The exact unit to which the victors belonged has never been established. Having been treated by the Red Cross, Daig recalls his first hours as a P.O.W.

"I was well treated after I was taken prisoner. An English Officer asked me if I had any firearms to which I replied 'no'. What surprised me was that he did not search me. I was then taken from the crash site to a nearby army base where I was shown to the commanding officer who offered me a glass of whisky. [It is likely that these men were from the 16/51st. Lancers or Royal Engineers who were, in 1940, based at the nearby Parham House]. I found such treatment comforting, especially after a defeat like mine".

One of those who caused the crowd of onlookers to swell was Mrs. D. Greenfield, having made her way over from her house in the Crescent in Cootham.

The large field behind the farmhouse forms part of the private airfield at Parham. Many of the eyewitnesses cannot recall the exact spot that the plane came to rest on the airfield, but the general consensus is that it was somewhere in the centre of the airfield. Once again, note the presence of Chanctonbury Ring in the background. (Authors collection).

"At about 5.45 I was in the garden when the plane in question passed low overhead with a Hurricane somewhere in the background. I made my way to the crash site on the landing ground by going along the main road from the Crescent and then in through the main entrance. I wanted to get to the plane so that I could get a piece of the Perspex from the windshield. All the children of my age wanted bits of this Perspex as we used it to make jewellery such as necklaces or rings. Unfortunately I had taken so long to get there that the army had already put a guard on the plane, and they were making it quite clear that I was not going to get my prize".

Another local resident also remembers his determination to "get a peek" at the crashed plane. At the time Colin Daughtrey was a 13-year-old schoolboy attending Rydon School.

"I heard about the crash from some of my school mates, and we decided to cycle and see the crash site for ourselves. I thought it would not be too much of a problem as it was on my way home. As I was then living at West Chiltington, this was of course the longer way home.

We cycled like mad and reached the airfield some 30 minutes after the plane had crashed. We approached the field from the south side - the main road entrance. We pushed our cycles onto the field and over to the crashed aircraft which lay almost in the centre of this large field. In those days there were many objects put all over the airfield; old carts, wagons, cars and anything the estate staff could lay their hands on. The idea was that this would prevent the Germans using the airfield for aircraft or gliders to land in an invasion - though on this occasion they were not very successful! .

The plane had made a belly landing and had apparently suffered little damage. All that we could see was the bent propeller. The aircraft looked quite new and had the typical black

cross on the side. We could also see the crooked cross on the tail fin. As we had arrived so late we did not get to see the pilot; the only military present were some armed troops accompanied by the local Policeman".

One of the many witnesses to the crash landing at Parham. As a 13 year old school boy Colin Daughtrey remembers cycling with his school friends to the crash site. He also recalls all the obstacles that had been placed on the airfield to deter an enemy landing - not that successful on this occasion! (Mr C.R.J. Daughtrey).

As with the previous crashes, Geoff Goatcher eventually arrived on his bicycle. He recalls a more detailed reason as to why Daig had crashed at Parham.

"I seem to remember that the plane had a bullet strike its oil tank which resulted in engine failure. The undercarriage was not

21

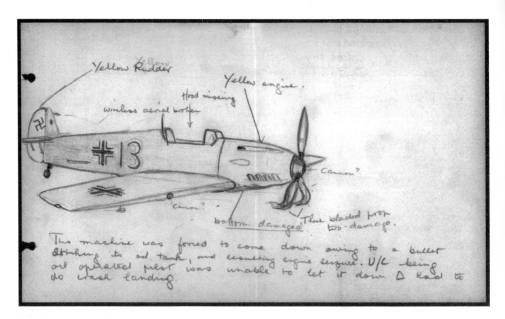

Drawing annotations:
Yellow Rudder
Yellow engine.
Hood missing
wireless aerial broken
+13
Cannon?
Cannon?
bottom damaged
Three bladed prop two-damaged.

This machine was forced to come down owing to a bullet striking its oil tank, and causing engine seizure. U/C being oil operated pilot was unable to let it down & had to do crash landing.

Geoff Goatcher's sketch of the Parham Bf-109. Again he helps to illustrate some of the damage caused in the crash, such as the bent propellers, missing cockpit cover and damaged engine cowling. (Mr G. Goatcher).

operable due to the fact that it may have been oil operated and hence the pilot was unable to lower it. I recall there being damage to the base of the engine cowling, two bent prop blades, and that the canopy was missing. The wireless aerial was also bent. The rudder and engine cowlings were yellow and the bar behind the white number thirteen on the fuselage was red."

Having seen the recollections of those local people who remember the crash, it is worth noting one of the official reports on the aircraft itself. Like Geoff Goatcher it states that the rudder and engine cowling were yellow, and that the aircraft codes of 13+- were white for the lettering and red for the dash. The report goes on to state that the plane had in fact been manufactured by Henschel and given their serial number 30155. The Luftwaffe serial or Werke number has never been properly established, some documents give this as 1488, whilst others 3488. The report concludes

that bullets had holed both the petrol tank and radiator, with further evidence of bullets hitting the port side of the fuselage. The armament was described as being standard, with one exception. The R.A.F. examiners found bomb release gear for four 30kg bombs at the bottom of the cockpit panel, with the release button located on the control column.

Paradoxically as a result of the aircraft's condition, Daig's Bf-109 went on to support the British war effort in its fight against the Luftwaffe. During the last months of 1940 dozens of towns and cities across the country participated in national 'War Weapons Week'. At the centre of many of these fund raising events were captured German aircraft, and in particular the Bf-109.

For about sixpence (2.5 pence) the public could stand and gaze at, or even climb into, a captured example of the Luftwaffes finest. In fact, during 1940 some 90 odd Bf-109s made successful forced landings in this country, many of which were snapped up by municipal authorities to be the centrepiece of their displays. It is known that Daig's 109 was part of these displays, having been photographed at fund-raising events in Birmingham and Dudley. It is quite likely therefore, that by crashing his aircraft as he did, Daig helped to fund part or all of the £6,000 that it was said a Spitfire cost to build!.

Following the Battle of Britain some 90 odd captured Bf-109s took part, in one form or another, in the War Weapons Week at the end of 1940. Oberleutnant Daig's 109 was no exception, photographed here on show in Birmingham. Following such displays, the majority of these fund-raisers were scrapped and the metal used in the allied aircraft industries. (Mr J. Hipkins).

FRIDAY 1ST NOVEMBER 1940

Officially the Battle of Britain had finished the day before the 1st of November, but the crashes did not end here. It was on this day that one of the worst plane crashes in the Chanctonbury area took place.

The plane involved was a Junkers Ju-88 from Lehrgeschwader (LG) 1. This was a mixed unit largely made up of former instructors and personnel of the pre-war German Technical Development Flying Unit. In November 1940 LG1 was deployed within VIII Fliegerkorps with its headquarters at Orleans/Bricy. The I and II Gruppen were based at Orleans/Bricy, whilst the III Gruppen were at Chateaudun.

The plane had been part of a large force of aircraft that had bombed the City of Birmingham, but on this occasion it fell foul of the anti-aircraft defences. It is thought that, badly damaged, the plane had turned south and headed back for Northern France. Gradually the plane lost height, so much so that it would eventually be unable to even clear the South Downs - this being the very reason why this Ju-88 came to crash alongside a quiet country lane in Storrington.

Junkers JU-88
GREYFRIARS

Aircraft Code: **L1 ✠ MB**

Werke No.:   4145
Flight Group: Lehrgeschwader (LG) 1
Crew: G. Reinnberg (pilot)
                G. Buseher, F. Pusehel
                W. Knaffe

The Junkers Ju-88 that crashed on the night of 1st November 1940 fell on the first day after the official end of the Battle of Britain. The site itself is literally next to the house called 'Faraday' in Greyfriars Lane.

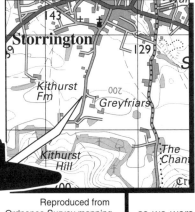

Reproduced from Ordnance Survey mapping with the permission of the Controller of HMSO © Crown Copyright, Licence no. MC 88223M

Ed Edwards was a soldier serving in the Canadian Infantry and who, in November 1940, was billeted at Fryern House, Storrington.

"On the night of the crash, we were some of the first people to reach the scene, having been ordered to attend from Fryern House by truck. On our arrival we found wreckage strewn everywhere from the houses in the lane out into the field and down the road. The wreckage blocked the junction at the front of one house, which I remember as we were unable to back the lorry up closer to the rest of the plane. I also remember something large, possibly an engine, which was still steaming up against one house.

From the crash site we could work out that the plane had been trying to fly over the South Downs to reach the channel. Being too low it literally hit the north side of the Downs at Storrington, between Greyfriars and Rackham Clump, bounced off the hill, nearly crashed at Coldharbour Cottages, before finally coming to rest in Greyfriars Lane.

We were tasked to remove the bodies of the crew back to Fryern House. It was whilst doing this that we found a pair of flying boots in the field - unfortunately complete with the legs chopped off at the knees. This most unpleasant task was made worse by the fact that light ammunition was still exploding in amongst the wreckage".

The Ju-88 had crashed at about 9.35pm in Greyfriars Lane, Storrington, almost on the doorstep of the house now called 'Faraday'. The wreckage spread from the field across Greyfriars Lane and did indeed reach the junction of the drive to Greyfriars House with the lane. The plane was completely wrecked, and three of the four crew dead. Unteroffiziers G. Reinnberg, G. Buseher and F. Pusehel were dead before Ed Edwards arrived, whilst the fourth remaining crew member, Unteroffizier W. Knaffe, was to survive though seriously injured.

Mr Waller also recalled the eventful passage of this plane across Storrington in the moments before the crash.

"As it lost the last few feet of altitude the crew ditched the bomb load that was still on the

A somewhat different illustration of a Junkers Ju-88. This is in fact a period illustration made from the original plates used in a local newspaper during the Battle of Britain. It shows a Spitfire attacking a Ju-88 over the Sussex coastline. Note the markings on the nose of the Ju-88. It is not known exactly what unit is portrayed here, but it maybe that the artist was attempting to portray the swooping eagle emblem of KG.30.   (By kind permission of the Directors of the Amberley Chalk Pits Museum).

The wreckage of the Greyfriars Ju-88, in the days following the crash. Here soldiers and airmen pick through the wreckage. What remains of the aircraft can be seen resting across the hedge and into the gardens on the other side of Greyfriars Lane. The telegraph and electricity poles on the left-hand side are still present today, and in fact give an exact location for the crash site.
(Mr A. Saunders).

One of the witnesses, Peter Bedlow. He recalls reaching the scene of the crash later on the same night, and finding the wreckage upside down. He also remembers that one of the aircraft's wheels was lying in the garden of 'Faraday'.
(Mr P. Bedlow).

This is one of the two wooden utility poles that can still be found at the crash site. It is said that as a result of the wreckage hitting these poles, they were gouged and scratched - damage which can still be seen today.
(Authors collection).

A photograph of the site as it is now from an almost identical position. Again note the hedge and wooden poles which are still present. Greyfriars Lane is just the opposite side of the hedge, and the house called 'Faraday' is on the left. (Authors collection).

The crash site as it is today looking south along Greyfriars Lane, Storrington, from the house now called 'Faraday'. On the right can again be seen the two wooden utilities poles that so clearly identify the exact location. The main wreckage from the Ju-88 rested on the right hand side of these poles, with a wing reaching across the lane and into the garden on the left. (Authors collection).

plane. About 6 or 7 bombs were dropped, and their location indicates the route that the plane had taken across the village. One bomb fell on West Chiltington Golf Course, one across Hurston Place, another on Hurston Lane, one straddling the A283 and one near my house. These bombs brought down the electricity and telephone lines in Hurston Lane. The next one hit the rear of my house, and its explosion damaged the roof and windows. My 3-year-old son was in a shelter under the stairs, and had he been in his cot I think he would almost certainly have been injured or killed.

The bomb that fell in the field near my house [Storrington recreation ground] failed to explode. The main road was closed and the army sent a bomb disposal unit. They located the bomb at a depth of about 14ft and it was subsequently removed on the back of a lorry. I remember thinking how the soldiers seemed completely unconcerned with the risks that they were taking".

Another member of the military that was slowly swamping the Storrington area by late 1940 was Peter Bedlow.

"In 1940 I was stationed in Storrington, with our Headquarters being a large house within sight of the Downs. It had a fairly steep drive at the bottom of which was a small lodge in which two or three of us lived [the big house is in fact Greyfriars House itself].

It was during one November night that an enemy aircraft crashed near the lodge in which I was then living. That evening I had been in the village itself and it wasn't until I was walking back that I noticed the commotion. When I reached the scene I found that the plane was upside down, and I immediately recognised it as a Junkers Ju-88. One of the aircraft's wheels was resting in the garden of the house that is now called 'Faraday', and as I had worked for Dunlop I noticed that some of the wording on the tyre wall read 'Dunlop Tyre Company'! It was a few days later that the wreckage was removed by the R.A.F., but at that time I was busy with my duties in the Headquarters".

As with all crashed German aircraft, a detailed report was submitted by R.A.F. staff. Their reports show that this Ju-88 carried the aircraft code L1+MB, with the 'M' in white. They went on to note however, that these markings had been painted over with black paint. There were also painted-over-letters to be found on the tips of each wing. The planes

28

upper surfaces were the usual dark green camouflage, whilst the under surfaces had been painted a pale blue. Both of the propeller spinners were green, though one carried an orange circle. Like the aircraft code, the Swastika on the tail fin had also been over-painted with black. The airframe itself had been built in June 1940 by Dornier, and carried the works number of 4145. Both engines were Jumo 211Bs made at Dessau. One of the engines revealed further detail in that it had been made in October 1939, and carried the serial number 47935.

As stated by many of the witnesses, the official cause of the crash given by the R.A.F. investigators was that the aircraft had been trying to land, and in so doing had hit a clump of trees. In the wreckage they were only able to locate part of the aircraft's armament along with a few large pieces of armour plate.

Ron Lampton owned the lodge that had been requisitioned by the army, and in which Peter Bedlow and his colleagues were billeted at the time. During November 1940 Ron was serving in the army and based in Wiltshire. His wife had moved out of the house and indeed was living away from Storrington. Ron first found out about the crash some time later when he picked up a Sunday newspaper and saw a photograph of the scene. Needless to say he instantly recognised the location. He remembers his initial comment to his colleagues - *"Cor, bugger me, that's my place in that picture!"*

Mrs Lampton recalls hearing about the crash

when she returned to live in the house. Local people said that the crew member who survived had been very young, and that he had spent the whole time asking for his mother.

One large lump of the wreckage had come to rest in the hedge that runs even now along the side of Greyfriars Lane. One of the wings lay across the road and into the garden of 'Faraday', whilst part of the fuselage rested against an electricity pole. It is in relation to this pole that the last reference to this crash can be found. At 8.06am on the morning of the 9th of November the Southern Region

A: This metal cover is still painted in the distinct 'battleship' grey that was used by the Luftwaffe and German aircraft industry during the war. It was found in 1990 by the author about 2 foot below the surface beside one of the wooden utility poles. It is thought, by virtue of the copper connector, that this item is connected with the aircraft's electrical or communication systems. (Authors collection).

B: Electricity board engineers dug up this piece of aluminium on the 28th June 1994. Whist investigating a local power cut, a trench was dug along the lane and in the process a number of pieces of wreckage were found. These are now in the care of the West Sussex Records Office at Chichester. (Mr R Ham).

C: More wreckage from the crash site. This time a piece of Perspex that was also dug up on the 28th June 1994 in Greyfriars Lane. The author and a local resident, Ron Ham, also have in their possession further examples of this Perspex. (Mr R. Ham).

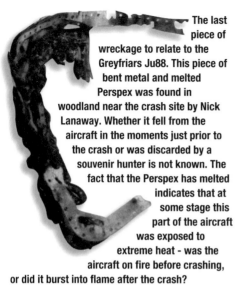

The last piece of wreckage to relate to the Greyfriars Ju88. This piece of bent metal and melted Perspex was found in woodland near the crash site by Nick Lanaway. Whether it fell from the aircraft in the moments just prior to the crash or was discarded by a souvenir hunter is not known. The fact that the Perspex has melted indicates that at some stage this part of the aircraft was exposed to extreme heat - was the aircraft on fire before crashing, or did it burst into flame after the crash? (Authors collection).

Headquarters of the A.R.P. contacted the Chanctonbury Area Control and enquired whether the electricity cables brought down in the crash had been repaired. In fact this memo gives the time of electricity loss as being 9.37pm exactly on the first. At 9.10 the Chanctonbury Control answered with the reply that the electricity cables damaged in the crash had in fact been repaired the same day.

This remark has further significance when an event, which happened in 1994, is recalled. During the hot summer of that year, the electricity supply to some of the houses in Greyfriars Lane was lost. The engineers who attended traced the problem to the electricity pole into which the Ju 88 had crashed. Having checked the fuses they were at a loss as to the cause, for their plans showed no joins in the cables that led from this particular pole. The current resident of 'Faraday', Ron Ham, suggested to the engineers that the crashed plane from some 50 years before may have been the cause. The workmen set to work digging up the cables, only to find an uncharted join in an underground cable about 7 metres from the pole. It appears that the wartime workmen had carried out emergency repair work on the electricity supply, but failed to update the plans!

Another shot of the wreckage at Greyfriars Lane in the days after the crash, showing military personnel beginning to remove the remains. The wooden utility pole in the centre behind the main lump of fuselage, is the one in front of which the round metal cover was found by the author in 1990. (Mr A. Saunders).

POSTSCRIPT

The air-war over the Chanctobury area did not cease on the night of the 15th of November 1940. The Chanctonbury Rural District was a large area, in fact it totalled about a sixth of the whole area of West Sussex, and for the remainder of the war aircraft and bombs continued to fall in sight of Chanctonbury Ring. This would include allied losses, as for example on the 10th March 1941, when a Spitfire of 616 Squadron dived into the ground near Wiston House. Its pilot, Sgt. Ben Bingley, was killed and now lies buried in the graveyard of St. Andrews Church, Tangmere. On the 29th March 1945, a Spitfire came down near Upper Beeding, this being the last of the 36 aircraft that crashed in the Chanctonbury area.

FURTHER READING

Bickers, R.T.   **The Battle of Britain - The greatest battle in the history of air warfare.**
                         Salamander Books Limited. 1990.

Burgess, P. & Saunders A.   **Battle over Sussex 1940.** *Middleton Press. 1990.*

Burgess, P. & Saunders A.   **Blitz over Sussex, 1941-1942.** *Middleton Press. 1994.*

Burgess, P Saunders A.   **Bombers over Sussex, 1943-1945.**
                            Middleton Press. 1995.

Haining, P.   **Spitfire Summer.** *W.H. Allen Co. 1990.*

North, P.   **Eagles High - The Battle of Britain.**
                        Leo Cooper. 1990.

Payne, M.   **Displaying the spoils - Captured German Fighter aircraft in the Battle of Britain.**
                        Aviation News, Page 398, October 1987.

Price, A.   **Battle of Britain.** *Arms and Armour Press. 1990.*

Ramsey, W. (Ed).   **The Battle of Britain - Then & Now.**
                        Plaistow Press. 1980.

Wood, D.   **Attack Warning Red.** *Carmichael & Sweet. 1976.*

ACKNOWLEDGMENTS

The research for this book has taken place over a number of years, in the course of which a number of people have provided invaluable help. In particular I must thank Geoff Goatcher, Andy Saunders and Pat Burgess, three people without whose help and time this book would not have been possible. I must also thank Peter Bedlow; Sheila Belcher; Mr Carpenter; Dr. Erwin Daig; Colin Daughtrey; Ron and Joan Ham; Andrew Hendrie; Mrs D. Greenfield; Joan Norton; Mr C. Turner and Ethel Woods (I would also like to thank my girlfriend Tracey for her never-ending support).

Many of the above people must also be thanked for allowing use of illustrations and photographs in this book. Once again I must make particular mention of Geoff Goatcher, Andy Saunders and Pat Burgess. My grateful thanks also go to the Directors of the Amberley Chalk Pits Museum; Peter Bedlow; Ron and Joan Ham; Dr. Erwin Daig; Colin Daughtrey; J. Hipkins; Wing Commander H. Randall D.F.C., Mrs M. Taylor and Jean Waller.